the Healing Habit

First published in 2016 by Columba Press
23 Merrion Square
Dublin 2
Ireland
www.columba.ie

IMAGE CREDITS

Photographs by Gerry Symes on pages 8, 13, 41, 44, 91, 97, 103
Photographs by Mary O'Shea on pages 26 and 71
Photographs by Michael Foulds on pages xi, 17, 22, 35, 51, 55, 61,
65, 77, 80, 86, 106, 113

Front cover photograph by Jan Tielens from unsplash.com

ISBN: 978-1-78218-308-2

Set in Abril 9/14
Book design by Helene Pertl | Columba Press
Printed with Jellyfish Solutions

the Healing Habit

DANIEL O'LEARY

CONTENTS

A WORD TO THE READER

The Healing Habit is dedicated to the human mind, with its sublime capacity to create the utter beauty of all that moves us so deeply, inspires us so profoundly, gives us the deepest pleasure. It also has the most terrible power to bring us immense darkness and unhappiness. The book is intended to honour and support you, the reader, as you search, with all of us, for the more abundant life, as you begin an exciting journey into a place that is brighter than you ever imagined, a place of dreams and imagination, of real possibilities, of a whole new way of seeing, and thinking and being. It was written so you would discover with delight what you were born to enjoy.

May you be blessed as you begin your courageous new journey, your decision to think differently and deeper. With hope, patience and perseverance you will soon notice encouraging changes in your life – a fulfilment, an enjoyment, a freedom. Keep this little book close to you always. Dip into it as often as possible to remind yourself of your goal, of your power to transform your life, of the love that fires and sustains your efforts. Grasp this special opportunity with great courage. Turn your life around. Follow your heart's desire. The important thing is that you actually begin now. 'Take the first step in faith,' wrote Dr Martin Luther King Jr., 'You do not have to see the whole staircase. Just take the first step.'

That is the desire of all those who readily and freely combined their time and talents to create this elegant, wee gem. Helene, Patrick and Michael of Columba Press gave it, as always, their sensitive and care-filled attention. Like an angel of grace may it fly into your world and transform it.

Slea Head, Dingle, Co. Kerry

*Let your new thinking begin with
facing your biggest fear.*

Trust the universe. It is full of love for you. Trust and believe. Above all, say 'Thank you' to the love, the energy, the wonder, the God you have faith in. There is a transforming power in that brief moment of gratitude. At the start of every morning, during all the daily preparations, keep repeating 'Thank you'. The thirteenth-century mystic Meister Eckhart said that if these were the only words you ever uttered, you would become a magnet for love and beauty.

THRESHOLDS OF THE MIND

There are hidden powers in your thinking. Befriend them and they will set you free.

THRESHOLDS OF THE MIND

Mind your mind. While you are awake you are constantly thinking. Your mind is forever creating the emotions you feel, even the kind of person you are. In fact, you *are* what you think. How you think is the key to your happiness. But because of the depth and stubbornness of your habits of thought, it takes much effort and time to identify, clarify and transform them.

There is another way of thinking, another way of seeing things, another way of living your daily life. You need to believe wholeheartedly that this is possible. Otherwise you won't have the determination, the courage or the motivation to persevere on this challenging new journey. It is a journey of hills and valleys, of light and shadow. Three brave and risky steps forward; two fearful safety-steps back.

But soon you will notice how much precious ground you are covering: each day a little more space, a clearer glimpse of the next step. And your weak and wayward mental patterns will slowly begin to surrender to the healing habit of your loving attention. Like a devoted mother, an alert guardian angel, you will begin to filter your every thought and feeling, discovering the hidden, negative ingredients that weaken your mind and deplete your energy. With the help of these pages you will quickly become accustomed to this essential, conscious aware-ness – like second nature. What you are not aware of you cannot heal.

TWO PATHWAYS – SPIRITUAL VISION
AND PRACTICAL STEPS

There are two interweaving pathways to the healing, strengthening and renewal of your life: the way of the soul and the way of the mind. Your soul and your mind are inseparable sisters.

First, the spiritual vision is about the loving trust that makes this transformation possible. It calls for a deep belief that we carry within us an invincible power, a sure conviction that we can make our mind like a faithful companion that will never betray us.

This kind of faith demands calm and constant vigilance. All the major religions carry this belief in their core teaching: that we are all travelling the journey to become very like the beautiful Creator in whose image we are made. This should give us great courage as we embark on the lifelong journey into the mystery of our true and deepest selves, because we will be tempted many times to turn back.

To avoid hopelessness, the daily torment of anxiety, the constant cloud of a restless, draining mental struggle, you need to believe in another gracious, healing context for your mind's safe thinking, another way of finding a new depth within you and around you. You need to acknowledge your powerful 'hidden self' (St Paul), the presence of an unspoiled and invincible sacred space in your deepest soul, a power and spirit that is the force and fibre of every word in this little book. It lies also at the core of our best healing courses, such as the renowned, non-religious twelve-step programme for those in the grip of addiction. And, as we will see, negative and depressive thinking is a form of addiction too.

This commitment to a deep and spiritual reality within will take you beyond your sporadic efforts, beyond your self-discipline and willpower, your new techniques of thought and your mental adjustments – though all of these will play a significant role as you set out towards your new horizon. There is a more profound backdrop, an inner compass for reaching your 'true north', the new destination for the rest of your life. The healing habit is more than a skill to master, an app to download; it is a beckoning horizon to reach, a lifestyle to adopt, a whole new world to inhabit.

What do I mean by this? I suppose such an understanding could be called a kind of determined trust, a fundamental belief, though you do not need to be 'religious' to possess it. It is what is missing from so many current mindfulness courses. What matters is that you have some idea of a strong, wise and loving spirit in the mysterious labyrinth of your heart, some notion of an ever-fresh well of life's sweet water within you, purifying, nourishing and energising your mind, your spirit and your body. 'If you keep a green bough in your heart, the singing bird will come to you each morning.' (Celtic wisdom)

Towton Battlefield, Yorkshire

The beauty of the world is silently calling for your attention – 'Think about me,' it pleads.

THE SECOND PATHWAY

The second pathway – the daily, practical work of the mind – is made up of the vital steps along the way that we need to take so as to keep moving towards our deeply desired destination. Most of these steps and suggestions are mentioned in the fifty-two insights of *The Healing Habit*. It is very important, however, to remember that any one of them, if embraced and practised, will somehow include all the others, and bring you safely home to that place of peace you long for.

As you set out on this new venture with its twists and turns, its cul-de-sacs and maybe unfamiliar signposts, here are a few general pointers to save you from getting lost too often, from losing your sense of direction, helping you to find your way without panic, to make the right choice.

Regarding every thought and emotion, endeavour to go in the direction of the positive, the courageous. There will always be risks. Get a sense of the direction of the wind of the Spirit of Life, and go with it. You will soon get a 'feel' for this; your deepest self has emerged from that same spirit. It will not lead you astray.

At that fleeting moment between thoughts, that brief space for grace when you have a chance to make a conscious decision about your next mental option, always try to make it in alignment with the loving forcefield of life, that basic energy that sustains and guides all things. You can call it the Source of Life, the Mother-Creator, the Gracious Mystery, God. Christians will call it the Holy Spirit. But, by virtue of being born, everyone on this planet possesses this astonishing gift.

The Lake, Kew Gardens

They are beautiful who think they are beautiful.

THE FALSE GUIDE

The mind is, of course, powerfully spiritual. Your beautiful mind, when fired by a loving trust, can transform your life at many levels. But your precious mind, when driven by greed, revenge, resentment or a burning sense of injustice, can wreak havoc on your inner peace and presence. And this virus touches all those around you, even the world itself. *What you do not transform you transmit.*

Notice also your strange compulsion to stray away from the safe path, to resist your true voice, to drift towards the negative, the closed, the deadly repetition of the same damaging thoughts and feelings. Deep in everyone's thinking there is a drive, a fatal attraction towards anxiety, towards giving up, becoming a victim of worry, or maybe towards getting even, being resentful, envious or judgemental. We usually keep this mental suffering well hidden from others. Most of our minds are more fragile and vulnerable than we let on.

These fatal forces are strong and persistent. They have been called the 'demons of the mind'. You may agree with those who describe them as addictions: those sinister patterns of thinking that bring so much misery and grief. Sometimes you feel powerless in their grip. For so many there is a kind of deadly attraction to their own flawed way of thinking and consequent feeling. They feel trapped in this condition, victims unable to escape.

Negative and anxious or fearful thinking devours our creative energy. It steals our strength and lessens our purpose and power. There is a worry-fatigue that eats into the resolve we need to grow and flourish throughout each day: a virus that infects the vibrant life of our imagination and beckoning dreams.

This is the false mind at work. The false mind is an illusion. It is not the truth. It is a relentless treadwheel of confusion. It holds you captive, preventing you from experiencing a new freedom from your anxious, self-protecting ego. That is why here, in this Part One, we have emphasised that, beyond sporadic efforts and programmes, useful as they may be, a more profound and deeper sense of the spiritual is needed for those apps and courses to work, for your courageous efforts to bear fruit, for the healing to happen.

Ennismore Retreat Centre, Cork

Do not fight or curse your mental pain,
hold it as you would hold a baby.

KEEP BEGINNING

In the light of the wisdom within these pages, and from deep within you, where the spirit lives, you will be guided in your new choice of a pattern of thinking: how to begin each day by preparing your mind for the many opportunities for growing and healing that await it; how to be faithful to the daily practice of continually expanding the horizons of your mind and heart, of untying those knots of a needless mental misery; how to stay open, to keep making new space for a blessed freedom to choose, at each and every moment, the true and loving way.

Later on in the book you will find the suggestion of taking time to envision the day when you will enjoy a happier mind, pre-experiencing it, anticipating the feeling of it, without the anxiety and depressive shadows that dim the light. This imagining of your desire puts added flesh and substance to merely thinking about, or half-hoping for that new day. Visualise the rich and positive reflections and feelings that will gush down the dry riverbed of your mind, the cool breezes that will blow across the deserts of your burning thoughts. Put all your longing and desire into attaining the kind of power and freedom and happiness that you envisage and visualise and you will gradually become that person.

This transformation of your thinking will demand your full attention, openness, surrender and cooperation with this healing, universal spirit. Without some special time each day to meditate on these life-transforming truths (begin with ten minutes), there is no point in beginning the journey. You need to soak the wisdom of the healing habits offered into your very being. That is why I have decided, throughout this small book, to occasionally re-emphasise some of the fifty-two key pieces of advice for the healing and renewal of your thinking habits, and to suggest one page, one paragraph for the whole week. (Though any one of them, if faithfully followed, may hold the key you are looking for.)

Without this attentiveness and repetition, you will forget what you have read, and the best part of your life may remain unlived. When you befriend your mind the rest of your life will be a new adventure. And your guardian angels love a new adventure. They will help you say 'yes' to your life with confidence each morning rather than hide from the challenges of another new day. *There is no better use of time than the re-creating of your mind into a well of joy.*

If you find something in these pages difficult to understand, just leave it for a while and come back to it later. Anything of real value will need several readings. And you will fail for a while. The mind is a stubborn part of us. But for heaven's sake do not give up. Turn over the next page and begin again. Every morning is another chance to continue. There is a divine energy in us that compels us to keep trying. Trust it. There is no other way. In 'Begin', Irish poet Brendan Kennelly wrote:

... Though we live in a world that dreams of ending
that always seems about to give in
something that will not acknowledge conclusion
insists that we forever begin.

Galtymore Mountains, Co. Tipperary

Get out of your mind and into your life.

Then one day I made an amazing discovery. I looked inwards and found I could tap into the bottomless well of strength which we all possess. In giving honest answers to myself I made the discovery that I was the architect of my own unhappiness ... I found that I changed my life for the better almost overnight. From this evolved my maxim: *We are the products of our own thoughts. We are what we feed our mind with. Change your attitude. Change your life.*

– 'Letters' Page', *Sunday Independent*, May 2016

Ballyvaloo, Co. Wexford

The love and freedom you long for, you already possess; they are ever only one good thought away.

See the things you want as already yours. Know they
will come to you when you open your heart to them
– 'Even before you pray' said Jesus. All great religions
know this secret of the mind. Think of what you deeply
desire as already yours, as belonging to you, as now
in your possession. And feel its presence. Sometimes
having a happy mind is as simple as that!

PRACTICAL, DAILY STEPS

Fifty-two insights, one a week, to mind the days and nights of your year.

1

Your way of thinking shapes who you are and what you become. You *are* what you think; you *are* the product of your thoughts. If you think hopefully, bravely, you become a brave and hopeful person. If you think fearfully, your eyes will betray you; you will become timid, anxious. Be prepared for a long journey, dear reader. But every day you will notice a difference. Begin by challenging the negative voice you hear in your head about your gifts and inner power. 'If you hear a voice within you say "You cannot paint" then by all means start painting, and the voice will be silenced,' wrote someone who himself knew how to handle a paintbrush: Vincent van Gogh.

2

Every morning you can make your day turn out the way you want it. If you think positively, believe persistently, prepare carefully and choose with confidence, then 'today will be a brilliant day'. This is the power of our thinking! There is a misery habit and there is a happiness habit. Do you realise you have a choice every moment of every day? You cannot escape the pain of living, but you do have a choice about how you handle it. You can give in and give up, or you can accept and grow stronger because of that pain. Suffering is a fact; how we see it is a choice. This is not to trivialise the power of pain. Making and persevering with this choice requires immense courage and effort.

3

You cannot plan the success of all your efforts but you *can* plan how to cope with the failures. And not just cope with them but become deeper and wiser *because* of them. You can play the alchemist: turning the lead of your mistakes into the gold of wisdom. You can play the optimist: turning the stumbling blocks of your days into the stepping stones to your dreams. Or you can play the defeatist: and lose heart. *You can change your destiny by changing your attitude*. This is a wonderful 'secret'; your mind will quickly make a habit of it.

Lake Superior, Northern Ontario, Canada

The worst bullies you will encounter are your own thoughts; almost all your anxiety is mind-made.

4

First-century-thinker Epictetus told us that nothing has the power to stop us when our minds are truly made up. At the 2015 BBC Sports Personality of the Year Awards (2000 years later!) Andy Murray and A.P. McCoy said that what you set your heart on will happen if you truly desire it, and make the necessary sacrifices to attain it. You can achieve all things! You can reach all your horizons. You can overcome all handicaps. You can forgive the greatest hurts, grow through the unkindest cuts. 'I can do all things in Him who makes me strong,' wrote St Paul. You are more powerful than you were ever told; you have an invincible power within you.

5

Your mind can be a delightful companion; it can also be a tyrannical controller. Thinking miserably is a habit; thinking bravely and positively is a habit too. Remember, we have a choice! The blind and inspired writer Helen Keller agrees: 'If we make up our minds that this is a drab and purposeless universe, it will be just that, and nothing else. On the other hand, if we believe that the earth is ours, and that the sun and moon hang in the sky for our delight, there will be gladness upon the hills and fields ... Surely it gives dignity to life to believe that we are born into this world for noble ends and that we have a higher destiny.' All of us can respond to our lives as we choose to. No one can take that precious freedom from us.

6

The human mind is powerful and wayward beyond measure. It can create joy from a 'bad' experience; it can create unhappiness from a 'good' experience. Please be aware of that. Your mind is a precious gift. Nourish it. Take care of it. It will serve you well. Most mornings I say to myself, 'It is my thinking that has the power to make me happy or unhappy today. It is utterly my decision. I have this one day ahead of me. No matter what, there is a way I can live it to the full.' Austrian neurologist Viktor Frankl wrote: 'When we are no longer able to change a situation, we are then challenged to change ourselves.'

7

Learning to think with power, passion and perseverance is the greatest grace. Mind your mind. Guard it from getting stuck in negative thoughts. *The price of a calm mind is eternal vigilance.* The trick is to catch yourself when your mind, unanchored, drifts off course into uncharted and troubled waters. Gently but firmly try to rid yourself of those negative thoughts at their first appearance; *that is when they are weakest.* Get into the habit of welcoming every morning like a child with a new look in her eyes. Each day is another opportunity to live and to love, to begin new things, to create something beautiful. With care and attention this will last throughout the entire day. It is the daily habit you were born for.

Flat Wood, Denby Dale, West Yorkshire

You have suffered enough in your mind;
it's time to come to your senses.

8

This attentive and vibrant way of looking at your life quickly becomes a blessed habit. St Paul reminds us: 'Summing it up, friends, I'd say you'll do best by filling your minds with, and meditating on, things true, noble, authentic, compelling, gracious; on the best, not the worst; the beautiful, not the graceless; things to praise, not things to curse ... Do that, and God, who makes everything work together, will work you into his most excellent harmonies' (Message Bible, Phil 4:8–9). Like second nature, the mind falls into this pattern of choosing what is healing and healthy for it. Some people read, watch and talk about the very same things, in the very same way, every single day. To the other 99% of ideas, possibilities, wonder and imagination, their minds are closed.

9

Your dream and your thinking, bring them together as deeply as you can. Weave your fragile dream into your patterns of hope-filled, optimistic thinking. Be always attentive and open to the Higher Presence. Millions rightly believe that, filled with a trust in a love that flows throughout the universe, they can think themselves into a happier life. They also know, as physicist Albert Einstein pointed out, they cannot change their worries by the same thinking that created them in the first place. But changing our ways of thinking takes patience, courage and perseverance. Some strange and strong forces within you are determined to drag you down. Remember the weird darkness in you that fights the light, that wants to crush your precious dream of a new beginning.

Antony Gormley's 'Another Place', Crosby

*The mind is a fire to be lit by wonder, not
a container to be filled with facts.*

❧ 10 ❧

Be prepared for a struggle, a kind of battle – even a kind
of dying – along the path of this journey to healing, health
and wholeness that you have chosen. This is the guidance
of all our wisdom traditions, our enlightened ancestors,
our religious elders. But they also encourage you not to
be afraid of the inner conflict, those dark forces, those
subtle demons of despair. In fact, in a most mysterious
paradox, those teachers all agree that it is often only at
the point of that persuasive temptation to quit that the
real dawn of a new perspective, a new way of seeing and
being, can emerge in the here and now. Pain, somehow,
is the teacher within; suffering, the hidden gift.

11

When things are not looking too good, risk opening your heart to courage: the courage to persevere, to stay on the difficult road for another mile. Do not turn back. Do not give up. The prize is priceless. You have glimpsed a wonderful secret. Do not forget. Leave no stone unturned. As Rumi wrote, 'Get up early. The morning breezes have secrets to tell you. Do not go back to sleep; do not go back to sleep.' One such secret is to start thinking lovingly, not judgementally; to perceive compassionately, not vindictively; to assess what happens to you with bigness and openness, not with a petty, stingy or closed mind.

❧ 12 ❧

Each day is a new day. This morning's thinking need not follow on from last night's distress. 'The past has no power over the present,' wrote spiritual writer Eckhart Tolle. There is a sublime freedom and energy in knowing that you can start each day anew. 'Sufficient for the day is the evil thereof,' the Good Book reassures us. Beginning your day in this confident fashion requires a definite and vital foundation: that of a healthy self-love. Without this basic and grateful acceptance of your own life, with its shadows and brightness, it will be impossible to muster up the energy to look with hope at the new day – especially at those times when your demons of doubt are hovering near.

𝕭 13 𝕭

You are connected with a positive and unfailing energy. In your mature thinking you can tap into the power of that forcefield of interconnectedness. You attempt to access this deeper, wider, wiser consciousness when you take time to be mindful, to meditate, to contemplate. This daily 10–15 minute habit of silence and stillness purifies, clarifies and untwists your tense thinking. You find the courage to renew your mind, to think with power, with confidence, with heart. You learn to give no oxygen to your toxic thoughts. Replace the poison of individual negativity with a healing compassion for all things. 'Let yours be great minds,' pleaded Pope Francis.

Kama Mountain, Northern Ontario, Canada

Your life is enchanted by the magic of your mind.

❧ 14 ❧

In spite of the terrible fear that grips the world these years, try not to say 'It's a bad world,' because it isn't. It is the beautiful body of its Mother-Creator. It is wounded, exploited and humiliated. But look for the positive. Think hope in desperation. Think beauty in a scenario of evil. And watch the difference your thinking brings about. In this way, you are a serious agent of change: in yourself first, then in our planet. American novelist Kurt Vonnegut wrote, 'Do not let the world make you hard. Do not let pain make you hate. Do not let the bitterness poison your mind. Even though the rest of the world may disagree, you still believe it to be a beautiful place.'

❧ 15 ❧

Your precious mind is precarious, vulnerable and prone to getting stuck in a vicious circle of repetitive negativity. Franciscan Richard Rohr writes, 'Almost all humans have Obsessive Compulsive Disorder (OCD) of the mind, which is why many people become fearful, suspicious, wrapped around their negative commentaries.' They become prisoners of their own thought patterns. In his *Eternal Echoes*, philosopher John O'Donohue writes about 'the crippling effect of our dried-out thoughts in the cul-de-sac of our minds'. To heal and recreate your mind you must learn to think in new directions and in different rhythms. That is what this little book is all about.

Galtymore Mountains, Co. Tipperary

The past is powerless over present possibilities.

16

Your beautiful, vulnerable mind is not to blame for your deep distress. Your mind is one of God's greatest gifts; the issue is *how you use it*. As well as their potential for wrecking your contentment, your thoughts possess an extraordinary capacity for transforming your life. It is not by trying to stop your thinking that you are set free, it is by *thinking differently*. You can change your difficult day by changing your attitude to it. You have this one day; why would you waste it? Every moment you spend paying a calm attention and discernment to what's going on in your head will be well rewarded. As St Paul advised, 'Let the mind of Christ be in you.'

❧ 17 ❧

How do we set about shifting the patterns of our mind? Albert Einstein wrote: 'The world we have created is a product of our thinking. It cannot be changed without changing our thinking.' When you do not succeed in shaping something to your liking then you can at least shape the way you think about it. You cannot escape the painful episodes of living, but you can *experience* them differently. When you change your habitual way of looking at things, the life you look at changes too. Unless you grasp this wise gift, and try to make it into a morning habit, you will stay stuck in negativity, quite unable to change the quality of your life. And remember, what we do not transform we transmit!

❧ 18 ❧

Much of your suffering is unavoidable, a necessary fact of existence. But how you *think* about it is a choice. This realisation is a moment of redemption. Otherwise, you stay victimised and diminished by your unanchored, uncharted and untrue thinking. You are defined by what you think. As within, so without. One cannot think fear and counsel courage, think dark and talk light, think crooked and walk straight. The light in your eyes and the energy in your body will reveal the quality of your mind. Again, remember, we have a choice here: to keep reaching, relentlessly, for the lovely light, or to give up the search.

❦ 19 ❦

As already emphasised, the main cause of your stress, in many cases is not the situation itself, not the things that happen to you, but the way you think about them. To repeat, you see things not as they are – objective, impersonal, neutral – but as *you* are – vulnerable, unsure, fragile. You mistake your fearful exaggerations for reality itself. This disturbing habit of falsely linking current disappointments and failures, real or imaginary, with past mistakes and embarrassments, accounts for most of our distress. We pile on more evidence about how useless we are, always mucking things up. Our self-esteem plummets. It is at this point that insecure people tend to panic.

Mazokama Bay, Northern Ontario, Canada

The inspiration of the truly thinking mind
is the same energy that turns our planet,
that fires evolution, that we call God.

❦ 20 ❦

Hamlet reminded us that 'There is nothing either good or bad but thinking makes it so.' There are hidden laws that order the patterns of the mind. One of these is called 'the law of attraction'. There is an extraordinary power in our persistent thinking about something we wish to have, or to avoid, that draws the imagined situation into our experience – for good or ill. This 'law' will deliver what your thoughts are focussed on. What you regularly, passionately, think about you bring about. You are desiring, creating, imagining a future state, and attracting that reality to you. Your quality of life – satisfying or unhappy – is the fruit of your thinking.

21

There is a story about two monks. The older one was making life impossible for the community's new member, criticising and ridiculing him relentlessly. As a last resort the young monk went away to meditate on the words of St Paul: 'Be ye transformed by the renewal of your mind and heart.' On his return he was, as he expected, immediately subjected to a hail of abuse from the older monk. 'And after all your time away from the community,' the older man spat out, 'and all the money you have spent, I still don't see you any differently.' The younger man paused, made space for a few breaths, slowly pushed back his cowl, turned to his accuser, smiled and calmly said, 'Maybe so, but I see you differently now.'

Gougane Barra, Co. Cork

Nourish your mind with the beauty
perceived by your heart and senses.

22

There is a spiritual dimension to the stilling and balancing of the troubled mind. It requires discipline and depth to harmonise our thoughts with the flow of grace, to enter the good energy of the turning world, to surrender to the timing and tuning of the Holy Spirit deep within. Every day we need those 10–15 minutes of deep time, still time, *kairos* time, when thought patterns are reconfigured, when a lost perspective is restored, when we connect with our essential self. There is a holy therapy in mindfulness, in meditation. John O'Donohue wrote that such reflection 'has something eternal in it. It is where we are most intimately connected with divinity. Thought is the place of revelation'.

❦ 23 ❦

With its capacity for goodness, truth and beauty, every human mind is potentially divine. Attuned to mystery, its longing for fulfilment is God's longing incarnate. But uncared for, it can destroy. It may lead us to the threshold of enlightenment or despair, of heaven or hell. The greater the gift the greater the shadow. Too many people live their later years trapped in a sense of regret, victimhood, bitterness. This is a real tragedy. Apart from childhood, there is no better time to enjoy a fully free, open, peaceful mind than in your middle and later decades. Make sure you begin to appreciate the power of your mind in good time! Everyone consulted in the production of this small book would advise you to *start now*.

❧ 24 ❧

Stripped of its spiritual, essential nourishment of quiet space and time, the mind will struggle to be still, to be wise. But when thought moves to the blessed rhythms of its true nature and grace, it deepens and flourishes. It finds its harmony when, in the stilling of your distractions, you connect with the underground river of the Creator's energy. This is a profound form of prayer; it brings a discipline, a direction and a spiritual connection to your patterns of thinking. And it spreads to others. W.B. Yeats wrote, 'We can make our minds so like still waters that beings gather around us so that they may see their own images, and so live for a moment with a clearer, perhaps even with a fiercer life because of our quiet.'

❦ 25 ❦

You are particularly vulnerable to distorted thinking when your self-esteem is at a low ebb, when you're experiencing a period of worry, when your thoughts begin to drift into negative and draining places. Gently shift your focus the moment you become aware of their toxic energy dragging you down that subtle slide into anxiety. Focus, for instance, on your breathing – just the awareness of breathing deliberately. Already you are moving from that unhappy place. Or simply pay attention to your senses – what you are touching, seeing, hearing – and slowly you are working free of that strange, strangling mental grip that is weakening your mind and body. Even a brief break each day from obsessive thinking will provide a healing space for recovering a lost balance.

Ballyvaloo, Co. Wexford

Mean thinking shrinks the soul, so think BIG.

26

Do not let your thinking victimise you. Careless, un-checked thinking brings much unhappiness. Becoming aware of it, and then changing this habitual, negative thought-pattern, will spare you much pain. But it takes time! Have you the patience to persevere? May I repeat this lesson? Spiritual teacher Eckhart Tolle wrote, 'We see things, not as THEY ARE (objective, impersonal, non-judgemental), but as WE ARE (anxious, vulnerable, very unsure).' The fearful mind can turn a trivial remark into a web of anxiety. Take this to heart. It will save you many hours of disquiet, mental pain and anguish.

27

You become what you think! Are you aware of what's going on in your mind? Do you pick and rake over old sores, scratching at the scabs of past hurts until they bleed again? Do you rush to conclusions, placing the most negative meaning possible on what happens to you? Are you aware that you are doing this or are you always trying to read the best possible meaning into your daily experiences, alive and tuned in to the interesting things going on around you, positively aware of what your senses are telling you? This habit is not always easy to acquire at the beginning, but it is a skill you will eventually master. You could begin by simply trying to be more mindful, occasionally, throughout your day, and then to deepen that awareness into a mind-nourishing way of being present at all times.

28

Do you eat mindfully? Do you walk, touch and look mindfully? Do you listen carefully to others, without interrupting their story? Are you one of those sensitive people with a thoughtful, care-filled attentiveness and respect that makes others feel safe, un-judged? Such mindful people are daily trying to find, nourish and live out their deepest self. Steve Jobs, Apple Computers co-founder, said, 'When the mind calms, it can hear more subtle things; that's when your thinking slows down, your intuition starts to blossom and you see things more clearly in the present. This is a discipline and you have to practise it.'

❧ 29 ❧

Your thinking has astonishing powers: to darken your
life or to make it radiant. May we remind you again (and
again!) that thinking constantly about something – good
or bad – is drawing that situation into your own experience. The mind is vulnerable to habit and repetition.
There is an extraordinary power in your thinking, in the
images of your mind. That is how you attract the light
or the darkness into your heart. Your thoughts become
your reality! *Times* columnist Sally Brampton, herself
the victim of depression, warned that 'your resentment
becomes your prison ... depression sucks the life out of
everything it touches'. And yet, she could add that compassionate thinking can restore our hope, our confidence
and the joy of life.

Northern Ontario, Canada

If you can dream it, you can live it!

✤ 30 ✤

Winston Churchill said that day by day we create our own universe. Your life, your happiness is in your hands. No matter what may have gone before, you can now change every situation in your life. As Jesus said, 'Whatever you ask for, you are already given it, *even before you ask for it.*' Whether you call it longing, prayer or deep desire, sooner or later your yearning will be answered, your hope fulfilled. That is the awesome gift of the mind. It is the way you are made. It is the divine power of your humanity. Humanitarian Helen Keller pleads with us to think powerfully, positively and confidently: 'Once, I knew only darkness and silence, before my heart leaped to the rapture of living. Your life will unfold for you as you expect it to.'

❧ 31 ❧

Beyond personal improvement, the healthy mind must spread outward, influencing and forming communities, weaving a deeper bond and sense of belonging among the neighbours. And beyond that local involvement, your mind, intrinsically connected with all life, is called to share that concern for the peace, protection and flourishing of the whole planet. Your marvellous mind, reflecting on the wonder-filled experience of an evolving world, is a vital forcefield of communication and inter-dependence at the heart of all being. St Paul, a champion of mind power, wrote to his friends of his desire 'to bind you together in love, and to stir your *thinking*, so that your *understanding* may come to full development, until you really *know* God's secret in which all the jewels of *wisdom* and *knowledge* are hidden'. Wonderful words.

Ventry Beach, Dingle, Co. Kerry

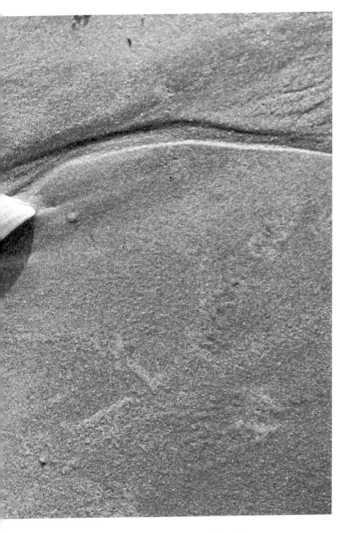

Once your mind glimpses a new idea, it cannot return to what it was before.

❧ 32 ❧

Your thoughts determine your feelings, your moods and your stress levels. Are you victimised or liberated by your thoughts and emotions? They play a huge part in your general wellbeing, in how fulfilled you feel. They can be the greatest cause of your happiness, or the main cause of your misery. It all depends on how you nourish your mind, or misuse and abuse it. Your fragile mind needs special care and attention. It is your best friend or your worst enemy. Nothing less than a full commitment to befriending and cultivating it will bring the happiness you seek. And as we keep emphasising, it will take patience and perseverance for this healing to become a habit.

33

'O the mind, mind has mountains; cliffs of fall, frightful, sheer ... ' Poet Gerard Manley Hopkins was well aware of the havoc caused when the mind is allowed to run wild, out of control, subject to false interpretations of our life's experiences. Your thoughts seriously confuse you when you fail to question the truth of what they are telling you. *Are my fearful thoughts true?* They can lead you into all kinds of doubts and misunderstandings, panic and low self-esteem. They heal and support you, bring life and hope to you, when you respect and nourish their power and giftedness, when you cultivate their extraordinary potential for living a happier life. Keep practising the habit of thinking yourself free. And do not lose heart!

❦ 34 ❦

There is a question we all need to ask ourselves: what is the difference between what happens to us, and what we *think* happens to us? What do we believe a particular event *means* for us? We need to learn to discern the ways we misrepresent reality through the patterns of our thinking. This misrepresentation, this false interpretation, often happens because of the power of our 'core beliefs' – those often-false 'certainties' we grew up with. Core beliefs can be positive or negative. They are like non-negotiable 'givens' even before we begin to think about some situation. They control, frame and determine the outcome of our thinking. Start asking yourself about how true they are. Question everything. Never be afraid to ask 'Why?'

35

Many ambiguous 'core beliefs' are brainwashed into us from childhood: about life in general and our own in particular, about values, about God, about religion, about right and wrong. They can skew the balance of good thinking. They act as a faulty filter through which we see the world, and interpret what is good and bad, what is a sin and what is not. Terrible damage has been done to our minds through bad education (indoctrination) and bad religion (spiritual abuse). This takes ages to heal because it makes us so fearful of our own truth and 'inner authority', of being different, of change. Are you aware of how you have been betrayed by those inherited deep-seated attitudes and 'certainties', how they have seriously limited your free and creative thinking?

Beaumont, Co. Cork

Sometimes our minds resemble a warzone,
sometimes a morning sunrise.

✤ 36 ✤

So much of your thinking is distorted. You come too quickly to false and negative conclusions about things. Your thinking has often been called 'addictive'. (This term is usually applied to substance abuse.) But there is also what is called a 'process' addiction which arises from the toxic pattern of your thinking, your habitual, subversive ways of reacting to things. Psychologists and spiritual teachers hold that a primary addiction for all human beings is the addiction to habit, to each one's own unexplored way of habitual thinking. Some people describe this persistent, diminishing experience as a form of 'possession' by the demon of destructive thinking. But courage! Even our most enlightened gurus have had to deal with their dark nights of the mind. That's how they know!

❧ 37 ❧

May we repeat that when everyone is thinking the same, no one is thinking very much. The addictive and noxious fear of change is seriously damaging the quality of your life. Without a lively, imaginative mind you stay helplessly caught in the tough tangles of your anxiety. 'Rake the muck this way. Rake the muck that way. It will still be muck,' according to Hasidic teaching. 'Would you not be better off seeing beauty everywhere you go.' To make mind-space and head-way you need daily spaces of stillness to become aware of what's going on within you. Zen masters call it 'wiping the mirror' so as to see exactly what's there, without distortion or false imagination, not what you *fear* will be there, or what you *want* to be there, but what is *really* there. *You wipe clean the mirrors of your mind and heart to see reality accurately.*

Ullswater, Lake District

*You cannot teach anybody anything but you
can help them to think openly and well.*

❧ 38 ❧

Spiritual teacher Richard Rohr holds that only when you see how self-serving, how petty, how narcissistic, how small and how compulsive your thinking is, only then do you realise how unfree you are. That kind of trapped, addicted thinking which 'possesses' you is healed only, he holds, by a more spiritual 're-possession' by a larger Vision, a belief in a greater Power, a greater and safer Love, a *huge* trust in the God of your heart. Until you have found your own ground and connection to the Whole Mystery (or whatever name you wish to use for it), you will stay anxious, fearful, unsettled, unsatisfied, grouchy, in danger of falling apart. 'Stay connected' is a constant refrain throughout this book. (Read Part One again.)

39

In your insecurity you are quick to believe the worst about yourself. Your self-esteem then is but a mere veneer; it is so easy to puncture your confidence. Try to stop jumping to false conclusions. Allow some breathing space to get a grip on your mind again. When you are in a negative pattern of thinking then most of your thinking is not true. Daniel Defoe said that the fear of danger is 10,000 times more terrifying than the danger itself. There are many variations on the story of the anxious person who, in the dim light, mistakes a rope for a snake and suffers agonies over it. And nothing will ever convince that person otherwise. We all have examples of such mistakes and harmful exaggerations in the course of our lives.

❧ 40 ❧

Identify with the higher, authentic, most beautiful soul given to you by your Mother-Creator from the beginning. It is the *real you* and lives in a safer place, stands on surer ground. It is free of any diminishment that can be done to you by others, or even by yourself. Protect it! Without your permission, anxiety and fear have no more power over you. Blame and anger and humiliation cannot possess you for long anymore. This is the *true self* that lives in the flow of free grace, the empowered 'soul' that can do all things because it is energised and inspired by the Spirit of Life which is God. Try to surrender to that spirit. Your body will tell you beyond doubt when your mind is in harmony with that *being*. Because then you will want to dance!

❦ 41 ❦

It is not by plastering over your negative thoughts with positive ones that you transform them. It is by courageously recognising their false substance, those 'core assumptions' that you have mistakenly taken as real and true. Look again at the cause(s) of your distress. Eckhart Tolle and Richard Rohr believe that most (85%) of your thoughts are repetitive, useless and damaging. This is so surprising; how deeply and constantly do we fall into the trap? Only the practice of meditation, of paying compassionate attention to everything and everyone, will guard your thoughts and feelings; the price of inner freedom is this constant awareness. Ask yourself for which pattern of your thinking are you providing most oxygen!

Nant Ffrancon Valley, Wales

*Your thinking can open thresholds of freedom
or it can imprison you in despair.*

❧ 42 ❧

'Come to your senses.' This is a well-known remedy for addictive, depressive thinking. We too easily get locked into the darkness of the mind. Try bringing all your beautiful senses deliberately into play, especially when out in nature smelling the white hawthorn, or rambling into your town's square. It is truly a delightful dawn when you wake up to the world of your senses and the clearer way of being and seeing that they bring. It is so deeply refreshing to discover those other natural ways of cherishing your soul. The Kerry-born mystic John Moriarty wrote: 'Bright mornings bring the mountains to my doorstep. Calm nights give the rivers their say. Some evenings the wind puts its hand on my shoulders. I stop thinking. I leave what I'm doing and I go the soul's way.'

❄ 43 ❄

You need to find other ways of thinking to reduce stress and a loss of perspective which leads to low moods or even some kind of depression. You need to stop believing everything you think, everything you were told. This is a shock for many. So much of your thinking is just not true. You must challenge it before it runs away with you, and you become locked into your thinking. How do you do this? Challenging your thinking is not just about bombarding yourself with forced, 'pretend happiness' to replace some misery. That won't help. But the best way is to courageously stay with the fearful, negative, stressful thought and reveal the lie in it, the assumptions behind it, its false core. That is how you transform your mind. And that is what these pages are urging and enabling you to do.

❧ 44 ❧

It is said that most people *become* their thoughts. They do not *have* thoughts and feelings; *the thoughts and feelings have them!* It is always a struggle to protect and nourish your essential and true self. If you do not live life, life will live you. For instance there may have been occasions when you felt ignored, wronged, personally humiliated. How did you react? Did you impulsively panic, jumping to seriously wrong conclusions about yourself? How long did it take you to get over it? It is vitally important to take time and space before responding. So often it turns out that you have completely misread the situation. And then, later, a perfectly acceptable solution or explanation is offered. In your haste, anxiety, uncertainty and insecurity you drew your misleading conclusions too soon.

❧ 45 ❧

There are people who find it almost impossible to stop thinking negatively, revengefully, darkly. They are obsessed, maybe possessed, by thoughts of being wronged, unjustly treated, bitterly blaming colleagues, family, religion, society, God. How can such people be helped to turn things around, to find a more true perspective on their lives, to regain a lost resilience, to re-make and re-mind their minds before falling into a state of despair? Is it possible for them to lift their habits of thinking to another level, from a kind of sluggish struggle to a brighter take on things? That is what *The Healing Habit* is attempting to do: to offer some solid ground for your walk to a happier life.

Flat Wood, Denby Dale, West Yorkshire

Solvitur ambulando: 'Take your mind for a walk.'

❧ 46 ❧

Can you identify some of the painful patterns of thought in your life? Do you resent the success of an enemy, the good fortune of a neighbour, the ordinariness of your own life? Do you still feel wronged by being passed over for the job you had greatly desired, or by your parents' will, or by the persistent memory of a false accusation? Do you suffer from low self-esteem, a sense of inferiority? For instance, do you ever tell yourself, 'I've done nothing useful with my life; I envy all those who are really clever, admired, who have a lovely family'? Do you take a critical remark and exaggerate it out of all proportion? Well, dear reader, if you answer 'yes' to any of the above questions, it simply means that you are a fairly normal member of the human race! But there is much you can do to lighten the darkness.

❦ 47 ❦

When the heart is grateful, the mind is healthy. When you appreciate who you are, enjoying the gifts within you and around you in your family, neighbourhood, nature, then the odds are that you are 'in a good place', responding in a balanced and positive way to the pain and wonder of your life. You may remember an old definition of prayer: 'a raising of the mind and heart to Love, to God'. Could you begin doing this? Thinking thankfulness. Practise the 'gratitude attitude', for the walk you've just had, the shower you've just enjoyed, the meal you are preparing, the friend who is calling in later, the friendly shop assistant this morning, the arrival of the email you were waiting for, the persistent demon you have finally befriended.

Ventry Beach, Dingle, Co. Kerry

Without a new breath you can live for a few minutes;
without a new thought you can live for decades.

48

We mentioned earlier the negative power of your misleading 'core beliefs'. Do you recognise any of the following? 'You think you need someone stronger and wiser than yourself to depend on. You believe that your past irrevocably influences your present, that you must pay the price for your mistakes, your sins. You are convinced that you have no control over your state of mind, that you are doomed to a life of anxiety, that you cannot change for the better, that you have no choice about how you live your life. You think that people do not like you, that they are watching you and talking about you, that they are always judging you.' It is so utterly important to identify, and then heal, these habits of the mind.

❦ 49 ❦

For many people, their destructive 'core beliefs' will have been implanted through religious indoctrination when small – with dreadful consequences. This brainwashing has been described as 'spiritual abuse', so great is the damage that has been perpetrated in the name of a church, an ideology, a God. Too many will have suffered grievously at the hands of a loveless institution that ruled by fear, that forced on young minds a horrible caricature of a hard, punitive God, who convinced innocent hearts of their badness, sinfulness, guilt and shame. Such damaged souls, whose creative gifts have never been nourished, find it so hard to think positively, hopefully, delightedly. They carry mental scars for decades. But even those scars will eventually yield to the healing graces of the healthy mind.

❧ 50 ❧

'A healthy mind in a healthy body.' As with everything worth achieving, there must be a complete commitment to the cause. In minding your mind you must also mind your heart and body. All parts of you interact with every other part. The way you think is affected by the way you eat, what you read, how you exercise, your alcohol consumption, the attention you pay to your breathing, your sleeping, the amount and content of TV you watch every evening, and how mindful you are in your choice of relationships. Without serious attention to these central lifestyle habits you can forget about any progress in the pattern of your thinking. Abundant information about how deeply these positive habits contribute to your mental hygiene is readily available.

❦ 51 ❦

In this small book we have discussed many central issues around the formidable power of your mind. But it is important for you to discover your own particular insights towards ensuring a lasting healing, energy and vitality. For many, for instance, there is a close and subtle connection between the state of their mind and the state of the surrounding environment. They need to have their affairs in order, and to be up to date with their work, before their minds can relax. Uncluttering their workplace, home, desk, diary or wardrobe, becomes, for so many, a key issue in the uncluttering of their minds, ensures a good night's sleep, and leads to a positive day's thinking. The habit of a greater order in their lives brings a healing freedom to their minds.

Kama Bay, Northern Ontario, Canada

We think too small; possibilities are endless.

❧ 52 ❧

The habit of developing an authentic presence among others, of mindful speaking, walking, eating and listening, gradually brings a confidence that nourishes healthy thinking. Comparing yourself with others is rarely helpful. Neither is defining yourself by your past mistakes. Be compassionate and tender with your struggling self; you have suffered enough. Talking things through with a friend is invariably a good way to regain perspective and clarity, as is giving your full attention to what you are doing. Anxiety comes from the unattended mind. And remember not to push yourself too hard to achieve everything at once. What you are seeking so desperately is already inside you, waiting for the moment to emerge. That is what this book is all about: preparing the ground, the circumstances, for that healing to happen, for that happiness to emerge, for a golden harvest to bless your life.